Tracing Our
IRISH
Roots

SHARON MOSCINSKI

John Muir Publications
Santa Fe, New Mexico

FRANKLIN PIERCE
COLLEGE LIBRARY
RINDGE, N.H 03461

John Muir Publications, P.O. Box 613, Santa Fe, New Mexico 87504
© 1993 by John Muir Publications
All rights reserved. Published 1993

Printed in the United States of America

First edition. First printing September 1993
            First TWG printing September 1993

Library of Congress Cataloging-in-Publication Data
Moscinski, Sharon.
American origins : tracing our Irish roots / by Sharon Moscinski
     p.   cm.
     Includes index.
Summary: Describes life in Ireland, the Potato Famine,
immigration to America, and the contributions of the Irish
Americans to their new land.
     ISBN 1-56261-148-8 : $12.95
1. Irish Americans—History—Juvenile literature. [1. Irish
Americans—History.] I. Title.
E184.I6M67 1993
973'.049162—dc20   93-2070
                                                             CIP
                                                             AC

Logo Design: Peter Aschwanden
Interior Design: Ken Wilson
Illustrations: Beth Evans and Nate Butler
Typography: Ken Wilson
Printer: Arcata Graphics/Kingsport

Distributed to the book trade by
W. W. Norton & Co., Inc.
500 Fifth Ave.
New York, New York 10110

Distributed to the education market by
The Wright Group
19201 120th Avenue N.E.
Bothell, WA 98011-9512

Cover photo, The Bettmann Archive
Back cover photo, Library of Congress

CONTENTS

The Bettmann Archive

LET THE JOURNEY BEGIN!

The United States of America is often called a melting pot of different nationalities. The idea of the melting pot is that people with very different ancestries, customs, and religions have assimilated, or "melted," into what is now American society. We all blend together. In recent years, Americans of many nationalities have become interested in their specific heritages and have sought to learn more about them. Although we are all one nation—one "pot"—this stew is made up of different ingredients, each unique. *Tracing Our Irish Roots* is a celebration of the Irish ingredient.

This book tells the story of the Irish American. It begins in the early 1800s, back on the Emerald Island itself. Most Irish immigrants came to America during the Great Famine. But even before the famine, over 250,000 Irish immigrated to this country. These immigrants were usually wealthy Protestants—often called the Scotch-Irish in this country—who left their homeland because they were dissatisfied with English rule. However, our story focuses on the Irish country farmers, who made up the majority of Irish immigrants to America. They are the forebears of most of today's Irish Americans.

NATE BUTLER

The voyage from Ireland to America was long and dangerous

How Many Irish Came to America?

Decade	Number
1820-1830	54,338
1831-1840	207,381
1841-1850	780,719
1851-1860	914,119
1861-1870	435,778
1871-1880	436,871
1881-1890	655,482
1891-1900	390,179
1901-1910	339,065
1911-1920	146,181
1921-1930	220,591
1931-1940	13,167
1941-1950	25,377
1951-1960	57,332
1961-1970	37,461

Between 1820 and 1850, the Irish made up about 42 percent of all people coming to America. Between 1851 and 1860, 35 percent of all American immigrants were Irish. After that, the percentage declined.

Girls and boys stroll down the street of a western Irish village in 1901

Irish farmers were jolly, boisterous, and energetic people. Deeply patriotic, they never wanted to leave their cherished homeland. But centuries of British domination had taken its toll on the Irish, and they wanted to be free. Under English rule, Irish Catholics, who made up 80 percent of the total population, were barred from almost every profession. All they could do was work the fields as poor potato farmers. When the potato crops began to fail, beginning in the 1830s, farmers struggled to feed their families. During the peak of the Great Famine, many Irish died of starvation. In desperation, masses of Irish fled their beloved country to America, to begin a new and better life.

During the Famine Years of 1845 to 1855, almost one million Irish arrived in the New York port alone. Hundreds of thousands more either anchored at one of the lesser ports in Boston, Baltimore, or New Orleans, or in Canada, and then traveled to the United States. The Irish made up the first large wave of immigrants to America. They were the first main ethnic ingredient in the "melting pot" that was to transform our nation.

Let us begin our journey through history. First, we will meet the Irish country peasants back in their homeland, where they struggled to stay happy despite English rule. Next, we will accompany the Irish through the days of the Great Famine, when a fungus destroyed their potato crops and forced many Irish to leave their beloved homeland. We will then sail with the Irish over the high, dangerous seas to the New Country. Here, we will admire the Irish as they remain strong despite poverty and persecution. Finally, we will cheer the Irish on as they gain political and social status, and at last are able to make the United States of America their proud and rightful home. So put on your sailor's cap, and let's go!

Farmers chat in their fields

3

FAMILY LIFE

Large, close-knit families were common in Ireland. Each married couple had between six and eight children, and often cared for their aging parents as well, whom they greatly respected. The Irish were taught, "If you are kind to your parents, you will have a long life." Even when it was nearly impossible to feed the extra mouth, the Irish would go hungry rather than cast aside a parent. "It's easy to halve the potato where there's love," the Irish would say.

The average family lived in a small mud or stone house with a thatched roof. There was rarely any furniture, and the family slept on straw beds. In the middle of the house was the hearth, the center of family life—and of famous Irish hospitality. Here, the family would sit in the evenings and eat, talk, play music, and tell stories. When visitors came, they were gladly welcomed, given the best spot in front of the warm fire, and offered a bowl of potatoes. Even during the Great Famine the Irish were generous. Their doors would be open to visitors, and they would sing, "We've an extra potato right hot on the fire, for one who may be passing through wet bog and mire."

The daily menu in Ireland included oatmeal, milk, honey, butter, and of course, the potato. After the autumn harvest, the potatoes were buried in a mound of dirt and peat to keep them fresh throughout the year. A family of six might eat over 50 pounds of potatoes a day!

Most Irish children were very healthy. They had rosy, glowing complexions, strong teeth, and suffered little from illness and disease. They were energetic, happy-go-lucky children who always knew how to have fun. But they also knew how to work and often helped with family chores. Whether they dug

The Bettmann Archive

Dancing the Irish jig

Irish youngsters had a carefree childhood filled with games, good times, and much family love. When the Irish were finally allowed to have their own school rooms, the children would march in and sing:

We'll go to our places,
And make no wry faces,
And say all our lessons,
Distinctly and slow;
For if we don't do it,
Our mistress will know it,
And into the corner
We surely shall go!

Library of Congress

Large extended Irish families typically lived in stone houses with thatched roofs

up peat for fuel, fished, hunted for snails, or gathered baskets of the many delicious wild berries that decorated the Irish countryside, they often made a game of it.

Parents tried to send their children to school whenever possible. The English had established many free schools throughout Ireland, but these schools were Protestant, and almost all the Irish were Catholic. Furthermore, before their lessons began, the Irish children had to recite this verse:

I thank the goodness and the grace
That on my birth have smiled,
And made me in these Christian days
A happy English child!

A happy *English* child? Proud Irish parents resented their children singing such songs. Although illegal, the Irish set up "hedge schools," so-named because they were held in secret behind large hedges. Screened from tattletales, the Irish children stretched out on the green fields and learned. Both girls and

boys were taught the three R's—reading, writing, and arithmetic—but only boys went on to learn geography, bookkeeping, surveying, mathematics, and Latin.

Library of Congress

Proud Irish parents cuddle their small child

5

IRISH COMMUNITY LIFE: FEAST DAYS

During the planting months in the spring and the harvesting months in the autumn, the Irish worked long hours tending their crops. But during the other seasons, they had quite a bit of free time. This time was often spent celebrating and merry-making.

Weddings were festive occasions. Girls usually married at 16 and boys at 17. It was only after marriage that young people were considered adults in the community, and weddings joyously celebrated this initiation. Family, neighbors, and friends were invited, and the ceremony took place in the house of the bride. Whiskey, wine, milk, and tea were offered, and the mother bustled about serving ham, fowl, bacon, soda bread, and other delicacies. Fiddlers played dance tunes and the Irish jigged and danced for many hours.

Fairs were also eagerly anticipated events, and people came to them from all over Ireland. Grazers sold their livestock, farmers sold their crops, and people discussed important issues together. The fairs also featured poetry, dancing, and athletic contests such as hurling, an exciting Irish pastime. Hurling was similar to a fast-moving hockey game, with almost no rules! Pushing, swiping, and quick reflexes were all part of the game—and suited the fiery Irish temper just fine!

Fairs were marvelous places to shop as well. In the booreens (alleys out of the way of traffic), canvas-covered tents housed such tasty foods as apples, gooseberries, plums, oysters, and boiled periwinkles (a type of snail). These treats were not usually available, and the fair-goers relished them. Children especially loved the fairs. They rode on merry-

Fairs were a time of fun and celebration.

The Irish thought nothing of walking 15 miles to a fair, but they did give a lot of thought to the superstitions of the day. Mother, father, and children would make their merry way down the road carrying salt, soot, or a sprig of hazel to protect themselves from evil spirits. If they passed a funeral, they took three steps backwards, and a woman was not supposed to whistle because it would bring bad luck to the listeners. But there were good omens, too. The Irish were very happy if they spotted a weasel or found a white button along the road, for that meant good luck for the entire journey!

WEDDINGS, FAIRS, AND

Sunday dinner with the parish priest

go-rounds and donkeys, attended awesome magic shows, and played games in which they could win prizes and sweets.

But the heart of Irish community life was the Catholic Church. Sundays were festive days. Families dressed in their very best and proudly paraded down to the local church. Afterwards, mothers prepared special dinners of meat or fish. The parish priest knew all of his parishioners personally, and a family was honored if the priest chose to dine with them.

Numerous religious feast days and festivals occurred throughout the year, and each one was observed with specific rituals and customs. For example, on St. Bridget's Day (Bridget is one of the patron saints of Ireland), families made crosses out of reeds, which were then sprinkled with holy water and hung throughout the house. Oats were thrown against the door to "drive away

hunger." And if a cloth, known as Bridget's cloak, was left outside, it was said to acquire magical healing powers.

Library of Congress

A jolly group gathers at the marketplace

MUSIC MAKERS AND STORYTELLERS

The Irish have always been great lovers of music, playing folk songs on harps, fiddles, pipes, or whistles. Some even learned to play beautiful music with just two spoons! In the 1800s, of course, the Irish had no televisions or radios, and most also had few books. Instead, they entertained one another with songs and music. Many an evening, large circles of children would laugh and sing to merry, sprightly folk songs led by family members. It was a great blessing to be a child in a musical household. If a child missed out on such an upbringing, the Irish believed no amount of money could ever make up for the loss.

When life was hard, the Irish often soothed their hearts by singing beautifully mournful tunes. And when times were good, they cheerfully sang and danced in celebration. The Irish were also fascinated with the supernatural; indeed, it was said that many of

The Bettmann Archive

Dancing the jig was a favorite Irish pastime

Peig Sayers (1873–1958)

Peig Sayers was one of the last of the great Irish storytellers. Her father was a well-known Shanachie. After the Great Famine, Ireland lost many tales of its culture and heritage when the storytellers died. Fortunately, Peig Sayers' stories were written down later in her life. Her folk tales, songs, prayers, and riddles filled 6,000 pages and, because of her, a great store of Irish folk history lives on.

The Irish were great music makers

A young Irish girl celebrates springtime

Courtesy of Harriet Blair

the old Irish families had fairies for ancestors. Numerous songs told of elves, sprites, or banshees, the Irish female spirit whose wailing warned of a death soon to come.

Another merry music maker who traipsed about Ireland was the "Come-all-ye." "Come-all-ye's" were ballad singers who would perform in the streets, in town squares, or at fairs. He or she would try to capture a wide audience by singing, "Come all ye lads and lasses" or "Come all ye faithful Irishmen." This is how the "Come-all-ye" got such a strange name!

Although the Irish loved music, an old proverb said: "A tune is more lasting than the song of the birds, and a word is more lasting than the wealth of the world." Storytelling was the favorite Irish pastime. Children and adults would sit by the fireside and listen to stories until the wee hours of the night. One Irish boy had learned over one hundred of these stories by the time he was only seven!

Irish storytellers had to have a good memory because their stories were not written down. They knew the stories from their own lifetimes, as well as the stories of the heroes from their ancestors, the Celts. The Celts spoke an ancient form of Gaelic, were generally farmers or warriors, and celebrated their religion with music, dancing, and ritual. Storytellers also had to be spry and inventive actors. The point was not to recite old tales word for word, but to color the stories with proverbs and dramatic expressions. Some tales made the audience laugh uproariously, but others were designed to give serious words of wisdom.

The kings and queens of the story-tellers were called Shanachies (SHAN-uh-keys). The Shanachies were not only the greatest storytellers, they were especially good at recounting the local tales, family sagas, and genealogies (histories) of their towns and villages. The Shanachies were the living history books of Ireland.

THE CLOUD OF ENGLISH RULE

The Irish were usually a lively, happy people. But a dark cloud always loomed over their lives. The Irish did not have their freedom. The English never viewed their Irish neighbors on friendly terms. They feared Ireland might someday conspire with another Catholic country against the English throne. They worried that Ireland would allow that country to use Ireland as a highway to invade England. England was also the more powerful country, and it knew it could forcibly take advantage of Ireland's natural resources for its own profit. So, in an effort to control and defeat the Irish, the English passed the terrible Penal Laws.

The Penal Laws stripped Irish citizens of all their basic human rights. Under these laws, Irish Catholics could not vote, work in the government, serve on a jury, become a teacher, study at a university, carry a gun, or enter many professions. They could not even own the land they worked on and improved over their entire lives. And when an Irish Catholic farmer died, he had to divide the land

In this political cartoon, Lord Salisbury tries to persuade England to oppress the Irish, and Gladstone tries to persuade England to let the Irish rule themselves

The Irish often outwitted the English with "blarney," the famous Irish art of double-talk. The tradition began in the 16th century when Queen Elizabeth tried to get Cormac Carthy, the Lord of Blarney, to admit that he owned his ancestral land only because the Queen herself had given it to him! Carthy hemmed and hawed and evaded her demand with random chatter until the queen exclaimed, "This is all Blarney! What he says he never means." From then on it was believed that if a person kissed a stone at Blarney Castle, that smoocher would receive the gift of eloquence!

Kissing Blarney Castle is said to give one the gift of eloquence

The Bettmann Archive

The police charge an angry Irish mob

he cultivated between his sons. But if one of his sons became a Protestant, he got the entire piece of land.

Irish Catholics were patriotic fighters who resisted English rule. Irish Protestants, on the other hand, had more in common with the English because they shared the same religion. The English hoped the harsh Penal Laws would convert fiery Catholics into friendlier Protestants. Here the Penal Laws failed; the majority of Catholics refused to change their religion.

But the Penal Laws did have a devastating effect on Irish society. Excluded from so many professions, what were the Irish Catholics, who made up 80 percent of the population, going to do? Those who broke the laws were punished by fines, imprisonment, public whipping, and sometimes even death. It was almost impossible to rebel against the British because the Irish upper classes, who had the power and education to unite the Irish people, had fled the country for their lives. The Irish peasants were abandoned, and alone had to suffer the pains of English rule. All they could do was farm. They

worked hard on the land of their own beloved country, but watched all the profits go to their English landlords. Often, toiling in the fields, they wished for a savior to free them from servitude. Their savior finally came. His name was Daniel O'Connell, and he was to become the hero of Irish independence.

A riot in Belfast

The Bettmann Archive

11

DANIEL O'CONNELL: AND COUNSELOR

I f an Irishman had been wronged, he definitely would not bring his case to the local authorities because they were either English landlords or their agents. The courts were even worse. The judges would often hang the Irish for even trivial offenses. The most notorious of these "hanging judges" was Lord Norbury. He once sentenced a man to death for stealing a watch. After telling the man of his fate, the judge laughed and said, "Ha-ha! You made a grab at time, egad, but you caught eternity!"

In 1792, the British Parliament passed the Catholic Relief Act, which allowed Irish Catholics to study and practice law. Daniel O'Connell was then a burly and boisterous 17-year-old from a middle-class Catholic Irish family. He chose this profession and, armed with its power, became the champion of Irish independence.

But being an Irish lawyer was not an easy task. The courts were controlled by biased English judges and Protestant juries. In order to be successful, O'Connell and other Irish Catholic lawyers had to be unusually clever and outwit the courts.

The Catholic Associations were funded by all the Irish. When in Dublin, the English novelist William Makepeace Thackeray observed: "Heaps of pence and bank notes told of the willingness of the people to reward their champion (O'Connell). The carboy who drove me had paid his little tribute of fourpence at the morning Mass, and the waiter who brought me my breakfast had added his humble shilling." These contributions, freely donated by a people who barely had enough to eat, totaled between twenty and fifty thousand pounds a year!

Daniel O'Connell (1775–1847)

The Bettmann Archive

The Bettmann Archive

THE LIBERATOR

Darryanne Abbey was O'Connell's country home

O'Connell filled this role perfectly. He was a crafty, daring, and often theatrical man. His keen oratory abilities often baffled witnesses into telling the truth. But he did not stop there. O'Connell bitterly resented English oppression, and so he began to use his skill with words to liberate his country right from the courtroom. Many a time, a simple case of who stole someone's cow ended with O'Connell railing against the evils of English rule, the glory of the Irish, and the tragic state of beloved Ireland. These theatrics were exciting and gave O'Connell a taste of power.

O'Connell began to use this power outside of the courtroom as well. Although all acts of sedition (activity against the English government) were illegal, O'Connell used his sly intelligence to overcome the law. For example, he formed various Catholic Associations to work towards Catholic Emancipation, an act which would allow Irish Catholics to represent themselves in British Parliament. These Associations were illegal, even when they just wanted to peacefully create a petition! Quick-witted, O'Connell had each member sign a document stating the Associations "were not representative of the Catholic body; nor shall they assume or pretend to be representatives of the Catholic body." Of course, such a statement was all "blarney," but it allowed the Associations to continue and flourish.

O'Connell's efforts created a buzzing underground political movement that unified the Irish and promised change for the future. And change did come. In 1829 the English passed the Catholic Emancipation Act, and O'Connell proudly took a seat in Parliament. O'Connell continued to make political advances throughout his lifetime, and when he died in 1847, he died a national hero.

THE IRISH FARMER

I rish farmers were tenant farmers, meaning they rented the land they worked, mainly from British landlords. Most of this farmland grew grain. Grain was as good as money because the tenant farmer used it to pay his rent to the landlord. The rest of the land was used to grow the potatoes, oats, cabbage, and other vegetables that fed his family and livestock.

The tenant farmer had no claim to any improvements he and his family made on the land. When it was time to renew his lease, if the tenant farmer had increased the worth of the land, the landlord could (and would!) raise the rent. This practice, known as "rack-renting," gave the Irish farmer little incentive to improve his land.

Farm laborers were even poorer than the tenants. Laborers were given a small plot of land to farm and a tiny hut to live in. In return, they had to work for the landlord a certain number of days out of the year. The landlord was very tricky. He might set the value of the house and the land at 30 weeks of work, but only use the laborer for 20 weeks. At the end of the year, the farm laborer would be deeply in debt, and the landlord could force him to remain on his estate.

Most British landlords were indifferent to their tenants' poverty and suffering. Many never even set foot on their Irish estates. Their chief concern was to make as much money as possible. To do this, they hired agents to manage their properties and see that the rents were paid on time. The agent had great power over the Irish peasant and was usually an unwelcome visitor.

A tenant farmer resists eviction

The Bettmann Archive

The Bettmann Archive

The Bettmann Archive

Prosperous farm families could afford cows and donkeys

Nevertheless, as long as the Irish had enough to eat, they would say they had a good life. But having enough to eat became more and more difficult. Between 1780 and 1841, the population of Ireland rose from 4.5 million to 8.2 million—an increase of 3.7 million people in just two generations! This population explosion dramatically affected the Irish way of life. What were these additional 3,700,000 people going to do?

They were going to do the only thing they could do: farm. The problem was that there was not enough land. Parents began dividing their land to provide for their children. But by 1841, the land had been divided so many times that over half of all farms were only one to five acres. Farms originally intended for just one family now had to feed as many as ten families!

No longer did each family have enough room for a small garden in which to grow different vegetables. Potatoes became the sole crop because they could grow in poor soil and small plots. In good years, just a few acres of

potatoes could feed a family of six all year round. But in bad years, the potatoes ran out. The summer months before the autumn potato harvest came to be called "the hunger months," and many families starved. You can see that the Irish were so dependent on the potato for food, if anything happened to destroy the crop, it would mean disaster for the whole country!

Library of Congress

A day at the sheep market

15

THE POTATO FAMINE

he Irish lived on the potato and little else. Each year they anxiously watched their potato crops grow and prayed for an abundant harvest. In 1845 the potato plants were blooming beautifully throughout the country, but it was rumored that a strange disease was causing potatoes to rot in England. Luckily, the Irish crops appeared healthy.

During the month of October, families worked long hours in the fields, shoveling up the large, tasty potatoes that would keep them alive all year long. Then bad news came. The potato plants, especially in western Ireland, had begun to rot into an oily, stinking, oozing mess! This was the only food many families had to live on. What were they going to do?

The Irish refused to be ruined by this calamity and began to prepare for a year without potatoes. They sold their livestock and belongings to purchase food, took extra care planting the following year's crop, and looked hopefully towards the future. "Feast follows

The Bettmann Archive

Women planting a crop of potatoes

A farmer discovers his potato crop has been destroyed

What caused this horrible potato rot? Fifteen years after the Famine ended, the enemy was discovered. It was a little mold fungus, similar to the one that causes mold to grow on stale bread. On a warm, humid day, the spores from just one fungus could produce millions of fungi! The fungi ate the potato plant. They multiplied so quickly, the fungi sometimes destroyed an entire potato field in just one night!

Mother and daughter sit beside the hearth

Library of Congress

famine," the robust Irish would say, and the next year's crop looked healthy. But the mysterious potato disease struck again, this time with full force. Almost every potato plant in the entire country rotted into a smelly, black slime. The Irish were seen beating their fists on the ground and wailing loudly as if they had lost a loved one. It seemed to them as if the land had failed them. They would have nothing to eat!

The potato rot continued to plague Ireland for ten long years. In desperation, the Irish turned to the English for assistance. The English sent two investigators to look into the situation, but they were little help. They advised the Irish to grate the rotten potatoes. The grated potatoes were then to be washed and filtered through a piece of linen. The remains, once baked, could then be mixed with oat, bone, or pea meal and used to bake bread. But how were the poor, hungry Irish, who had no graters, linen, ovens, or meal,

supposed to follow these directions? How could they be expected to eat food that would make them sick?

Finally, the English were pressured into taking some action. They decided to build workhouses to aid the poor, establish soup kitchens to feed the hungriest people, and grant funds for a Public Works program so the Irish could earn enough money to buy food. But these projects were expensive and the English did not really want to help the Irish. In newspapers and cartoons, they often characterized the Irish as drunken, stupid beggars. One politician even claimed the famine was God's punishment for the Irish who stubbornly remained Catholic! Because of their prejudice, the English relief efforts were half-hearted and ineffective. They did not want to pay to keep the Irish alive.

17

LIFE DURING THE GREAT FAMINE

It is hard to imagine how terrible life was for the Irish during the famine; it is remarkable they had the will power to stay alive. Some rummaged through the fields and ate any berry, weed, or leaf they found. Others, too weak to forage for food, were filled with despair. Although there were many fish in the sea to eat, the Irish lacked the boats, fishing lines, and nets necessary to catch them. Instead, they plunged into the freezing waters to gather seaweed. Eventually, even all the seaweed had been eaten. One traveler reported seeing "little children leaning against a fence—for they could not stand—their limbs fleshless, their bodies half naked, their faces of a pale greenish hue—children who would never, it was too plain, grow up to be men and women."

Men had to leave their wives and children to look for work in England or in one of the workhouses scattered about Ireland. But usually there was no work, and when there was, many men were too weak from starvation to lift their tools above their heads.

The Bettmann Archive

In this 1880 drawing, the desperate Irish look toward America for relief

Library of Congress

Often, the landlord removed the thatch and "tumbled" the cottages of his tenants who could not pay rent

Amazingly, while millions starved to death, thousands of tons of grain were being shipped *out* of Ireland and *into* England! Grain was not affected by the fungi that devastated potatoes, and if the tenants who still had their farms did not pay their rents in grain, they would be thrown out of their homes.

The Bettmann Archive

Thousands of hungry Irish beg for food outside of a workhouse

They were not fed enough at the workhouses, either, and many died. The women and children who had been left alone were helpless and hopeless. All they could do was beg for food at soup kitchens. But the soup kitchens had too many people asking for food.

The winter was cold, and the Irish had pawned all their warm clothes and blankets. Thousands were homeless. As a result, people would sleep in crowded rooms to keep warm or in the workhouses, which were filled three times over their limit. These conditions led to the final straw in the famine crisis: disease began to sweep through the country.

The Irish, unable to wash, were riddled with fleas and lice. Lice carried awful diseases, such as typhus. Once infected, typhus victims would develop a very high fever, their faces and lips would turn purple, and they would usually die within two weeks. In such crowded conditions, typhus lice could easily jump from head to head, and typhus spread like wildfire throughout Ireland.

Starvation was a visible death that took a long time. Typhus, however, was invisible and killed quickly—and even worse, it was contagious. "Will I catch typhus?" everyone asked in terror. Sick of hunger and fed up with disease, the Irish wanted out! America was their only hope. Literally, they ran for their lives.

By 1855, over one million people—over one-eighth of the total population—had died of either famine or disease. Things were only getting worse. The Irish had a choice—a dismal one, but a choice. They could either leave their homeland or die.

FAREWELL, BELOVED IRELAND!

The Irish did not want to leave their homeland. Their lives were hard, but they loved their land. On the eve of departure, their minds were filled with memories of better days. Days when the land was generous and harvests were plentiful. When Mom pulled the ears of naughty children, only to hug them to her chest. When Grandma sat churning butter outside the cottage, recalling the days of long ago, when she too twirled and frolicked till midnight at the country dances. When Father came home sweating from his hard toil in the field, took his place by the fire and said, "Ah! It's good to be with my family and eat my evening meal!"

But the Irish, especially the young, had to leave. Ireland could no longer offer them a future. Country girls impatiently awaited marriage, but Irish lads had neither the land nor the means to support a wife and family. Young men thought about their future and wondered when their hard work would earn them a better life. And of course, the Irish who

Emigrants prepare to board ships bound for either New York, Boston, or Quebec

A ship leaves beloved Ireland

How did the Irish pay for their journey to America? The fares were inexpensive, but any money was too much for the Irish peasant. Relatives already in America often paid for the tickets of Irish family members, but more commonly, the landlords sent their tenants to America. Why? The English had passed a law that required the landlords to pay for the relief efforts during the famine. The more people on his estate, the more the landlord had to pay. In the long run, it was cheaper for the landlord to ship his tenants over to America than it was to pay for the relief efforts! This twist of fate allowed many poor Irish to make the voyage to America.

Emigrants say their final goodbyes to family and loved ones

were completely wrecked by the famine, who had been thrown out of their homes and were unemployed, would die of starvation or disease if they remained. These Irish wistfully looked at the fields of their homeland for the very last time, and left with a heavy heart.

On the brighter side, emigration was an exciting adventure. Even before the Great Famine many Irish, tired of English rule, chose to try their luck in America. Naturally, they wrote to their families back in Ireland about their life in the New World. "In America," the letters read, "wages are high, work is plentiful, land is cheap, everyone can vote, and people can afford to eat meat everyday." What? Work, food, land, and freedom? This seemed too good to be true! Girls and boys, women and men, and sometimes whole families packed up the few belongings they had, and braved the wide Atlantic in search of a better life. As their ships began to drift away from the family and the land they would never see again, they sang:

Ireland is Ireland through joy and through tears,

Hope never dies through the long weary years.
Each age has seen countless brave hearts pass away,
But their spirit still lives on in the men of today!

The Irish could be forced to leave their homeland, but they could never be forced to give up their feisty Irish ways. The Irish would bring all of their "Irishness" with them to America!

The Irish had high hopes about the New Country

CROSSING THE WIDE ATLANTIC

Traveling to America was a nightmare during the Famine Years. Thousands upon thousands of Irish desperately wanted to emigrate, and shipping companies tried to pack as many people as possible into the dingy area below deck called steerage. Little concern was given to the comfort or safety of these unfortunate people.

The Irish immigrants could sail to the United States on either American or British sailing ships. The American ships had been designed to carry passengers. They were cleaner and faster, and were stocked with adequate supplies of food and water. But they were also more expensive. The Irish who could not afford the higher fares had to ride on the British ships instead. The British ships were designed to carry lumber and cargo, not people.

Nevertheless, the shipping brokers promised the Irish travelers decent conditions

Sailing away to the New Country

on the British ships. There was even a law, the Passenger Act of 1842, that guaranteed each passenger one quart of water and a half-pound of food each day. Unfortunately, however, there were no inspectors on board to make sure the passengers were being properly treated.

Instead, the Irish were forced to live in nightmarish conditions. They found themselves crammed into dank, rotting, unseawor-

During the Famine Year of 1847, one out of every six passengers died on the British ships. (In the same year, only one out of every 145 people died on the American ships.) One historian wrote, "If the route from Ireland to America had been a highway, it would be lined with crosses marking deaths along the way." Sadly, these immigrants were the victims of the same hunger, disease, and death they sought to escape in Ireland.

Steamships were cleaner, safer, and faster than the sailing ships

Immigrants take a break on deck from their airless quarters in steerage

thy vessels. The steerage compartments were filthy. There was no place to bathe and there were no ventilated toilets. The stench was nauseating and disease was a constant threat.

Water shortages caused additional problems. The ships' crews always took plenty of water, but doled out stingy portions to the hundreds cramped in steerage. Sometimes, the Irish immigrants were given such tiny amounts of water they drank only a few sips per day. With no water, the Irish could not eat their provisions, which were preserved with salt, because it was impossible to quench the violent thirst that followed. Even on board the ships, the Irish went hungry.

The British shipping companies rarely required medical exams. Usually, the immigrants were considered healthy if they could walk on board. As a result, many sick people were allowed to travel. With the sick sleeping between the healthy in the crowded, dirty compartments, disease ran wild. Many immigrants died from disease on their way to America, and the sailing ships became known as "coffin ships."

Diseased and hungry, the passengers felt completely hopeless. Many immigrants began to wonder if the voyage was worth it after all. It is easy to imagine, then, how excited the passengers became when after eight, nine, or ten weeks of travel, land was sighted at last. Was it true? The Irish rushed up on deck to see for themselves. Yes! The Irish had finally arrived in America!

By the mid-1880s, the Statue of Liberty greeted ships sailing into New York Harbor

Library of Congress

ARRIVAL IN THE NEW COUNTRY

The Irish immigrants exited their ships and gazed wide-eyed at the land they were to call their own. The immigrants who had relatives to greet them were lucky; they picked up their trunks and left to join the established homes of their fellow countrymen. Most Irish immigrants, however, had to fend for themselves in a strange country. They knew little about the customs, prices of goods, money exchange rates, or means of travel in America. They were very vulnerable.

These Irish were bombarded by "runners" who hung around the immigrant ports. Runners worked in cahoots with crooked rooming-house keepers. The runner would grab hold of an immigrant's baggage and trot away through the crowds. With the baggage as ransom, the runner led the bewildered

The immigrants land in New York

immigrant to a rooming-house, where he was pressured into renting a room. Both the runner and the rooming-house keeper would then charge the immigrant outrageous fees.

Immigrants were often warned about the runners, but they had little chance to protect themselves. As soon as a ship docked, as many as 400 runners would jump on board and seize the immigrants' belongings. One hapless newcomer had two runners take off with his belongings, each in a different direction! He decided to follow the runner who had his most valuable possessions.

Irish Americans helped new immigrants make their way in the New Country

There were some efforts by the Irish themselves to soften the perils on shore. Many Irish-American women made a habit of going down to the ports to make sure the Irish newcomers, especially young girls traveling alone, were not taken advantage of. Also, the Irish Emigrant Society of New York reported cases of wrong-doing, and helped Irish immigrants get on their feet in the New Country. But with thousands arriving every day, these efforts could only help a small percentage of the immigrant population.

Castle Garden welcomed the thousands of immigrants who arrived each day

Some runners lured newcomers by parading around as Irishmen themselves. They would fake a heavy Irish brogue, wear a shamrock on their hat, and assure many a skeptical Irish immigrant that they were comrades from the "auld country." They offered places to stay (at ridiculous prices) and assisted with travel plans. One such character sold a luckless immigrant a ticket for $145 that should have cost only $8.60!

The runners were disliked by everyone, but they could not be controlled because the ports were so crowded. In New York, efforts were finally made to ease immigrants' arrival in America. New York's Castle Garden became the official port of entry for all immigrants (until Ellis Island opened in 1892), and the runners were barred from entering.

At last, newcomers could land in friendly, well-organized ports. They were able to buy good food at reasonable prices and were guaranteed fair rates of exchange for their money. Their luggage was protected from thieves, and a list of honest, inexpensive rooming-houses was posted. Unfortunately, the largest waves of Irish immigrants came before Castle Garden was established. But for the immigrants who arrived after 1855, the first days in America held promise, not just hardship.

Scoundrels known as "runners" snatched the immigrants' luggage as soon as they docked

THE IRISH WORK FORCE

When droves of Irish reached America during the 1840s and 1850s, they were welcomed to a country that was still mainly rural in character; only about 15 percent of the population lived in cities. The arrival of the Irish helped create an abundant work force that allowed the country to grow and expand, and cities began to flourish.

Although most Irish immigrants were farmers in the Old World, they were ill-suited for this profession in the New World. They preferred to live side by side with their fellow countrymen in cities and towns rather than pioneer the wide, lonely, land-locked prairies of America. Besides, Irish farmers used only a spade and a simple plow. They were not familiar with the advanced farming methods used in the United States. With little money and no skills, all the Irish had was their willingness to work.

The Irish became the strong arm of America, and the physical strength of their masses turned overgrown towns into thriving cities. The Irish helped build roads, sewers, water systems, bridges, and new housing. They were seen swinging their picks and heaving their shovels throughout the streets

Irish women could immigrate as easily as their brothers because they could support themselves working as chambermaids, nannies, seamstresses, or cooks for rich "Yankee" families. Irish women were often harassed about their race and religion—in one case a miffed nanny poured a bowl of soup right onto her tormentor's lap! But they were also appreciated for their cheerful attitude, strict moral standards, and willingness to work for low wages.

Library of Congress

Immigrant women working at a doll factory

Library of Congress

National Archives

Irish clam diggers in Boston, 1882

of America. One newspaper remarked: "There are several sorts of power working at the fabric of this Republic—water power, steam power, and Irish power. The last works hardest of all."

However, even the major projects to expand the cities could not employ the thousands of Irish who streamed into the country daily. As a result, the Irish were recruited to join "work gangs." The work gangs tackled the country's more ambitious projects. The Irish became the diggers of the Erie, Champlain, Chesapeake, and Ohio canals. They became the coal miners in the dark caverns of Pennsylvania. They became an essential part of the indispensable force that built the railroads across the country.

The work gangs were forced to do dangerous work, and if a man was injured or killed on the job, his family received no compensation. The canal diggers who worked

knee-deep in swampy waters often suffered from cholera, dysentery, and malaria. Coal miners toiled in unsafe mines and were frequently buried alive in cave-ins. And railroad work was so dangerous, it was said that an Irishman died for every tie laid down on the railways. Newspapers were littered with stories of "Paddies" being crushed by beams, killed in explosions, or maimed in accidents. (Paddy was a common Irish name and soon became a nickname for Irish immigrants.)

To add insult to injury, the Irish were habitually cheated by their contractors as well. For example, the Irish often worked in remote areas and were forced to buy provisions at extremely high prices. Paid only $1.00 per day (plus a ration of whiskey), many an Irishman became bitter. With famine in the homeland, perils on the journey, and hardships in America, many Irish wondered when, if ever, they would have a better life.

LIFE IN THE SHANTIES

The Irish were determined to make America their home. However, because they had very little money and needed to live close to their jobs, the Irish were forced to move into areas that offered inexpensive housing. Consequently, Irish "shanty towns" sprung up in almost all the Eastern cities, where large groups of Irish immigrants settled.

The shanty towns consisted of hundreds of run-down, overcrowded structures. Greedy landlords divided warehouses, factories, and large buildings into small, cramped, unsafe apartments. They then charged their Irish tenants outrageous rents. A stuffy basement apartment cost about $6.00 per month, which was quite expensive in the 1850s. But since this was cheaper than housing in the

Neighbors stop to chat

better neighborhoods, and the Irish were eager to live among other Irish immigrants in the unfamiliar American cities, they were stuck in the slums.

The buildings in the shanty towns were fire hazards and poorly heated in the cold winter months. The water was tainted, the unsanitary conditions were terrible, and trash lay out in the streets to rot. Not surprisingly, the shanty-dwellers were ravaged by disease. In one Boston slum, one out of every 17 Irishmen died in 1850! Saloons popped up on every corner, and the crime rate soared.

Although Irish immigrants were poor, they often had large, warm families

Close familial bonds are characteristic of Irish families. As late as 1960, Irish American families ranked number one in the amount of time parents spent lavishing affection on their children, but also in the amount of time scolding. Warm, loving, yet strict Irish families have remained a mainstay in American family life.

New York Historical Society

An Irish shanty town in Central Park, New York

Although the shanty towns were falling apart on the outside, they were both home and haven for the Irish on the inside. The city streets bustled with activity and the home buzzed with affection and love. Neighborly good will and generous hospitality remained faithful Irish traits, and during harder times, the Irish helped one another out within the community. Family life changed little from the Old Country. Mother still sewed, cooked, and raised a large Catholic family. Father toiled for long hours with his pick and shovel, and came home to have his pint of beer in an easy chair. Children played in the streets rather than the Irish fields, and boys joined neighborhood gangs. The Irish even kept livestock with them in the American cities! Pigs slept side by side with family members just as in the days of old. At one time, they even became a public nuisance when over 10,000 pigs roamed the streets of New York!

One difference from the Old Country, however, was that Irish men died young in America. Forced to work 12- to 14-hour days in strenuous jobs, Irish men usually died in their thirties or forties, and left their families without an income. When such a tragedy occurred, the Irish community banded together and collected a "purse" to help out the fatherless family. Afterwards, the awesome strength of the mother, often called the "widow woman," kept the family unit together. The younger children were kept in school, but in their spare time they peddled papers, ran errands, and rummaged through junkyards for items that could be mended or sold. The older children, sometimes only 12 or 13, quit school and took on full-time jobs to support the family. The "widow woman" became a deeply respected figure both by her children and the Irish community.

IRISH GHETTO CULTURE

The Catholic Church was without a doubt the central figure in the Irish community. Disgruntled priests immigrated to the United States right alongside their parishioners, and together they struggled to establish a thriving religious life in America.

Initially, there were no churches in the Irish shanty towns. The Irish, although very poor, had to pay to build the churches themselves. When the community church was finally completed, it was a source of great pride for the Irish because it had been built by their own efforts and sacrifices. Church activities were an important part of neighborhood life, and they further bonded the Irish together in a hostile Protestant environment. The priests were friends with their parishioners, and they sympathized with the hardships they were forced to endure. The Catholic Church not only promised the Irish salvation in the next world, but soothed their weary hearts in this world as well.

The neighborhood saloons hustled and bustled with activity. They were the meeting places, political areas, and fun-houses of the Irish community. Here the tipsy Irishman, surrounded by the sing-song of his familiar brogue, engaged in heated arguments about politics, poked fun at his swaggering companions, or just drowned the sorrows of his cheerless life with one too many beers. In these "poor man's clubs," the Irish sang, laughed, and were temporarily relieved of the misery that often plagued their lives.

But a drunken Irishman is a rowdy Irishman. Passionate shouting matches and hot-headed fights were common barroom scenes. Crime and public disturbances were often caused by Irishmen who had had too much to drink. The red-nosed, swearing, fighting, drinking Paddy became an unfortunate stereotype. It was said that, "Many of the Irishman's troubles and much of his unfavorable reputation are directly traceable to too great a devotion to the bottle." And when one man confessed to drinking too much, his priest warned, "You must take care, my son. Drinking is a problem we Irish have."

The Irish organizations, militia companies, and firemen were famous for staging theatrical parades on national holidays. Each group would, with competitive pride, try to outdo the others in ceremony and splendor. It is no wonder that the St. Patrick's Day parade in New York City is one of the most elaborate parades in the entire country!

St. Patrick's Day was a fun-filled day of celebration

The Bettmann Archive

A typical tenement room in New York City

These concerns prompted Father Theobald Mathew to crusade against "Demon Rum" throughout the country. Although he persuaded over a half-million Irish to sign a "teetotaler," a pledge not to drink, the saloon remained an unshakable fixture in Irish communities.

To replace the fading tradition of storytelling and music making, the Irish also founded many organizations designed to unite the community outside of the home. The Ancient Order of Hibernians and the Knights of Columbus sponsored benefits and fundraisers. In Boston, the Charitable Irish Society and the Shamrock Society made St. Patrick's Day a holiday filled with pride and fanfare. The Irish militia companies probably existed as an excuse to have dinners, banquets, parties, and parades! However, the most thrilling of all the Irish alliances were the fire fighters. In the Irish ghettoes, fire fighting was done by volunteers, and it was a point of honor to be the first company on the scene. Sometimes "fire laddies" even battled stubbornly over the use of a lone fire hydrant while the building steadily blazed on.

National Archives

An officer inspects a basement apartment

PREJUDICE

In the mid-1800s, America was not a very diverse society; most of the citizens were Protestants of British descent. Many Americans believed the immigrants coming to the United States threatened the established American way of life. Because the Irish were the largest immigrant group at that time, they bore the brunt of American hostility.

During this time, established American citizens—commonly called "Yankees"—were often intolerant. They were not used to foreigners and were distrustful of lifestyles that differed from their own. And the Irish differed quite a bit from their Yankee neighbors. One journalist remarked that it was difficult to imagine two "more incongruous elements" than the "jolly, reckless, good-natured, passionate, priest-ridden, whiskey-loving, thrift-less Paddy, and the cold, shrewd, frugal, correct, meeting-going Yankee."

In particular, Americans criticized the Irish for being "clannish." But the Irish lived together because they shared a common lot. Furthermore, they needed to band together if they were to build a community Church and send their children to Catholic schools.

The Americans were also scandalized by the filthy Irish ghettoes. They saw illiteracy in the homes, crime in the streets, and a saloon on every corner. And gambling and prizefighting, although illegal, were nevertheless favorite Irish pastimes. As a result, most Yankees viewed the Irish as lazy, drunk, gambling, hot-tempered hoodlums. They blamed the Irish for transforming their clean, safe city streets into overcrowded and filthy slums.

In addition, the Irish were willing to work for low wages, and the competition in the job market made it more difficult for Americans to find work. Even more frightening to the Yankees, the Irish were steadily gaining political power.

Anti-Irish and anti-Catholic sentiments began to sweep through the nation. Jobs were regularly advertised with the clause, "No Irish Need Apply." Jokes, stories, and hurtful stereotypes about the Irish were common.

Irish women seeking employment were discriminated against just as much as Irish men. The following advertisement was typical of the 1850s:

Woman wanted—To do general housework . . . English, Scotch, Welsh, German, or any country or color except Irish.
—*Daily Sun*, May 11, 1853

"No Irish Need Apply"

Irish immigrants were frequently portrayed as rowdy drunks

Irish children were treated unfairly in the public schools. And Protestant ministers began a crusade against the Catholic Church.

These activities gave rise to a new political party called the "Know Nothing Party." The Know Nothings wanted to keep political power out of the hands of immigrants, especially Catholics. The party got its strange name because when questioned about their activities, members replied, "I know nothing about it."

This party gained considerable strength during the 1850s. A favorite trick of the Know Nothings was to use violence to prevent immigrants from voting at the polling booths. Baltimore was known as "mob town" for its election-day battles and bloodshed, and many immigrants were torn from the voting lines and beaten.

Prejudice against the Irish only grew. The Irish were repeatedly harassed and their Catholic churches and convents were vandalized, set afire, and even bombed. The angry Irish retaliated against these abuses, and riots became common city scenes. Fortunately, the Know Nothing Party quickly lost power after the 1850s and violent, racist activities against the Irish became less common.

Immigrants were frequently harassed at the polling booths

PROFILES OF THREE IRISH AMERICANS

John L. Sullivan (1858–1918)

Their spirited, feisty character made the Irish Americans ideal fighters, and many an Irish immigrant gained fame using his fists. The most famous prizefighter was John L. Sullivan, a Boston Irishman who, although of only medium build, had powerful fists said to have "the kick of a mule in them." After working in a variety of jobs (he had even studied to be a priest!), he went to a boxing exhibition at the Dudley Street Opera House in Boston. A well-known local fighter named Tom Scannel boasted he could beat any man who dared to challenge him. Sullivan accepted this dare and knocked Scannel senseless.

Sullivan began touring nationwide, offering $50 to anyone who could remain in the ring with him for four rounds. Undefeated, Sullivan went on to beat Paddy Ryan in a heavyweight championship match so famous the playwright Oscar Wilde covered the story for a British magazine. Sullivan remained the heavyweight champion for ten years. He became a national legend, but an Irish American hero. In 1887, the city of Boston honored Sullivan with a diamond and gold belt that was 4 feet long and 1 foot wide. But in 1892 Sullivan was finally defeated in 21 rounds by another Irishman, "Gentleman Jim" Corbett. "The Boston strong boy" never fought again, but he was also never forgotten. When he died on Feb. 6, 1918, thousands lined the streets of Boston to honor their hero.

Library of Congress

Heavyweight champ John L. Sullivan

Cardinal James Gibbons (1834–1921)

Cardinal James Gibbons was born in Baltimore in 1834. At age three he returned to Ireland, where his father died of fever during the Great Famine. In 1853 he came back to America and settled in New Orleans with his mother and siblings. He decided to enter the priesthood and eventually became one of the most important American figures in the Catholic Church.

During Gibbons' time, the American scene was changing rapidly. Catholics were entering politics, labor unions, social reform groups, education, and other professions. The Church needed to expand and to address the changing lifestyles of its parishioners. Gibbons' strength was diplomacy. He was able to make effective changes without compromising the Catholic Church. Gibbons supported the rights of laborers to form unions and condemned child labor. He worked hard to embrace all other immigrant groups into

Mary Therese McCarthy, a 20th-century novelist and critic

the Catholic Church (which originally was almost entirely Irish), and to make the Church respectable in a Protestant America. Gibbons was made a Cardinal in 1887, becoming the second American to receive this distinction. He was honored nationwide, but it was said, "Although he reigned in Baltimore like a king, he met every man like a comrade."

Gibbons was the second American to become a Cardinal

Mary Therese McCarthy (1912–1989)

Mary McCarthy was born on June 21, 1912, in Seattle, Washington. Her father was a successful, second-generation Irishman, and her mother was a Protestant-Jew who converted to Catholicism soon after her marriage. However, orphaned as a child, McCarthy was sent to live with relatives who, she said, "had a positive gift for turning everything sour and ugly."

Nevertheless, McCarthy became one of America's leading novelists and critics. She wrote about politics, education, and the role of women in America, and championed her causes with satire and brutal honesty. For example, McCarthy wrote in later years, "My belief is nobody believes in God any more except peasants and simple people; the others just pretend to." Not surprisingly, such sweeping statements often provoked anger, especially among the religious Irish Catholic community. Nevertheless, McCarthy remained a respected intellectual until her death in 1989.

The Bettmann Archive

Library of Congress

THE IRISH IN THE CIVIL WAR

In the mid-1800s there was a movement to abolish slavery. Many Americans understood that the institution of slavery was wrong and shamed a nation that promised freedom to all of its citizens. But the Irish were generally opposed to this abolition movement. They feared the freed slaves would take away the few jobs available to them. Furthermore, the Irish had so many problems in their own community, they could not be sympathetic to the problems black people faced as well.

But when Civil War ripped the country in half, President Lincoln declared that the purpose of the war was not to free the slaves, but to save the Union. The Irish were first and foremost proud Americans, and they objected to the Confederacy's attempt to secede from the nation. They eagerly enlisted in the Union Army.

Between 150,000 and 170,000 Irishmen joined the Union ranks. The Irish Brigade, which consisted of Irish regiments from New York, Pennsylvania, and Massachusetts, became the most famous and feared of all the Irish units. The heart of this green fighting machine was the celebrated

---

The battlefield united the Irish and the Americans under the common cause of saving the Union. The only distinctions were between North and South, and all soldiers were fiercely loyal to their own side. One Confederate soldier ordered an Irish color bearer (flag carrier) at gunpoint to "Hand over those colors, Yankee." The surprised Irishman replied, "*Yankee* is it now? Faith, I've been twenty years in this country and nobody ever paid me the compliment before!"

Library of Congress

Recruitment poster for an Irish regiment

Library of Congress

Library of Congress

Irish-American soldiers fought bravely in many important battles, such as the Battle of Fredericksburg

69th New York Regiment, led by General George Meade and Captain Thomas Meagher.

The Irish regiments won the respect of their fellow Americans with their heroics on the battlefield. They were key figures in all of the major battles, especially Antietam and Fredericksburg. During the Battle of Fredericksburg, the Union suffered terrible losses. However, the Irish regiments fought so courageously, Robert E. Lee himself later said of their efforts, "Never were men so brave. They ennobled their race by their splendid gallantry on that desperate occasion. . . . Their brilliant assault on our lines excited the hearty applause of our officers and soldiers."

Unfortunately, the Irish stained their favorable image back in New York City. Two years into the Civil War, enlistment in the army became compulsory, not voluntary. The Irish could not afford the $300 fee to avoid serving, so they made up the majority of men drafted into the Union Army. When the war to save the Union turned into a war to free the slaves, with Lincoln's Emancipation Proclamation, many Irish no longer wanted to fight. Angry Irishmen launched a bloody four-day riot targeting innocent blacks. The Colored Orphan Asylum was burned down, and blacks were beaten, murdered, and hanged by Irish mobs. At least 300 people were killed. One author commented, "It was a classic example of the poor in their misery venting their fury on the poor who was even worse off."

Overall, however, the Civil War established a new level of national unity. The Irish soldiers returned to their cities not as poor immigrants, but as national heroes. Prejudices melted on the battlefield as the Irish risked their lives to save the Union, and the "Paddy" and the "Yankee" became brothers in arms.

MOVING UP: ADVANCES COMMUNITY

The Irish were entitled to a right in the United States they were denied in Ireland: political power. And they exploded onto the American political scene with a bang! Success in politics required charisma, street-smarts, and "skilled oral dueling," and the Irish reigned in all three areas. They also took advantage of their great voting power as a group. As the Irish loyally voted for politicians from their own neighborhoods, politics became the only career in which it was an asset to be Irish!

By the late 1800s, the Irish dominated big-city politics in the Eastern cities. The leaders of these political rings were called "bosses," and they had to be tough, shrewd, friendly, and generous. The bosses were all self-made men who were born and bred within the city slums. They learned about politics in the neighborhood saloons, made connections, and climbed their way up the political ladder.

The Irish bosses wielded their power to overcome discrimination and make headway for the Irish community. First, they squashed anti-Catholic prejudice practiced in prisons and schools. Next, they appointed Irish Americans to jobs in education and public service. Finally, they created work within the Irish community by funding the construction of schoolhouses, subways, and bridges.

The Irish were also instrumental in forming labor unions. In the late 1800s, work gangs, miners, and unskilled laborers began striking throughout the country. They learned that as a unified group, they could demand better pay and safe working conditions. The union trade movement arose to organize these efforts, and many Irish emerged as union leaders.

The Irish also rose in social status as new waves of immigrants flocked to the United States. These immigrant groups now stood underneath the Irish, and so pushed the Irish a few rungs up the social ladder. As the Irish were already the bosses, union leaders, and policemen of working-class commu-

Library of Congress

Al Smith, the 1928 Democratic presidential nominee

One Irishman who captured the political spotlight was Al Smith of New York City. He rose from the city slums to become governor of New York from 1918 to 1926, and in 1928 he was the Democratic Party nominee for the presidency of the United States. Although Al Smith lost the election to Herbert Hoover, he was the first full-blooded Irish Catholic to strive for America's highest political office.

IN THE IRISH

Mary Harris Jones, popularly known as "Mother Jones," was an influential labor leader. For five decades Mother Jones spoke out eloquently in favor of better wages and working conditions for laborers in the cotton and steel mills, coal and copper mines, garment industry, and railroad yards.

Library of Congress

nities, they became the natural middle-men between the newly arrived immigrants and the established Yankee society. In fact, to the new immigrant groups who could not even speak the language, the Irish seemed quite Americanized! Indeed, one Czechoslovakian woman who had a difficult surname to pronounce complained, "I used to wish I had an *American* name like the kids in our school who were Kellys and O'Briens and Sullivans!"

By the 1930s the Irish had become common figures in politics, unions, and police stations. They were represented in banking, insurance, industry, entertainment, publishing, and education, and they were more successful than any other immigrant group at the time. Second and third generations of Irish Americans increasingly finished high school, and the wealthier families sent their children off to college. By the 1930s, the Irish could finally sigh with relief. For most the worst was over, and the struggles of the past were only hand-me-down memories of former generations.

The Bettmann Archive

Tammany Hall was the Democratic Party's New York City headquarters and the political arena for many Irish-American bosses

JOHN F. KENNEDY

John F. Kennedy was born on May 29, 1917, in Brookline, Massachusetts. His mother, Rose, was the daughter of the Boston politician John "Honey Fitz" Fitzgerald, and his father, Joseph Kennedy, was an ambitious, wealthy businessman. He often dreamed that one of his sons would one day become president of the United States.

John F. Kennedy began his career as a commander of a motor torpedo (PT) boat stationed in the Pacific during World War II. He barely escaped death. A Japanese destroyer, the *Amagiri*, smashed the PT boat in half, killing two men instantly. Kennedy performed many heroic deeds to get his men safely to shore, but still they were marooned in dangerous enemy territory. Luckily, some friendly natives hid Kennedy and his men in their longboats, covered them with palm fronds, and paddled them past the Japanese guards to safety. Kennedy's actions earned him the Navy and U.S. Marine Corps medal of heroism.

When John F. Kennedy returned from the service, he became very active in politics. He served in the House of Representatives for six years, and in 1952 defeated the popular incumbent Henry Cabot Lodge for the United States Senate. Kennedy spent his political career crusading for better working conditions, more public housing, higher wages, and civil rights legislation. He became enormously popular. Finally, in 1960, John F. Kennedy was elected the 35th president of the United States. He was both the youngest man and the first Roman Catholic ever to do so.

Kennedy's victory was an enormous boon for Irish Catholic Americans. Ever since they set foot on American soil, Irish Americans had been key players in the theater of

Kennedy inspired the nation with his speeches

The Bettmann Archive

While in Berlin, Kennedy famously ended a speech by saying, "Ich bin ein Berliner." Kennedy thought he was saying, "I am a Berliner." But he had actually said to the German people, "I am a jelly donut." ("Berliner" was the common name of a jelly donut!) This blunder was undoubtedly very funny, but his genuine effort to speak to the people of Berlin in their own language earned the president much respect.

Kennedy shares a moment with his son, John F. Kennedy Jr.

politics. However, there was a widespread belief that a Roman Catholic candidate could never be elected president. Kennedy's victory squashed that belief; there was no longer a limit to what Irish Americans could achieve.

Kennedy captured the heart of the nation with his Irish-bred charm and his rough-and-ready charisma. He was an intelligent, avid reader and a rugged athlete (he popularized "touch" football). He set an example for Americans to exercise both their minds and their bodies. And he mesmerized the nation with his speeches. John F. Kennedy inherited the Irish eloquence that had produced countless bards, storytellers, and orators. His speeches were spirited, patriotic, and visionary. Kennedy summoned the nation in his inaugural address to "ask not what your country can do for you; ask what you can do for your country." In 1961 he rallied the nation to meet the challenging goal, before the end of the decade, "of landing a man on the moon and returning him safely to the earth."

The nation was stunned when it learned that their president had been assassinated. On November 22, 1963, while riding slowly through downtown Dallas in an open limousine, Kennedy was fatally shot in the back of the head. The whole country, especially Irish Americans, mourned his death greatly.

John F. Kennedy (left) with his younger brother, Robert F. Kennedy

CONCLUSION: THE IRISH AMERICAN

Although there are now many laws that make immigration into the United States difficult, the Irish continue to come to America. These new immigrants are generally dissatisfied with the lack of opportunities in the southern part of Ireland, or are fleeing from the ongoing war in the north, and wish to try their luck in the "New Country." Irish newcomers are often welcomed into this country by Irish Americans who are still interested in the welfare of Ireland. In fact, a large number of Irish Americans are very concerned about the problems Ireland faces today, and help out wherever possible.

Unfortunately, as we have seen, it was not always easy to be Irish American because prejudice against the Irish was enormous for many years. Often, Irish immigrants could only escape ridicule and become accepted members of society by giving up their Irish ways. And indeed, many Irish Americans shed the customs, behaviors, and quirks that made them a unique ethnic group.

Understandably, it upsets many Irish Americans that they have lost so much of their ethnic heritage. As a result, an increasing number of Irish Americans are educating themselves and their children about the history and culture of Ireland, and are learning Irish Gaelic, the language of the Irish people before English rule.

Although we are all Americans, each of us may rightfully ask, "Where did I come

Immigrant children adapted most easily to American ways

Library of Congress

From priests to politicians, Irish Americans have entered every profession

from?" We should be proud of our ethnic roots! Our roots, directly or indirectly, have not only contributed to who we are, but also to the character and strength of America.

The Irish are an American success story. They came to this country without power or possessions, but with plenty of spunk and spirit. They made a point of gaining political power and, once armed with this power, went on to dispel anti-Irish prejudice and to demand their rights as full citizens of the United States.

The Irish had a head start over the other immigrant groups who came to America later. The political, religious, and social advances won by the Irish made them ideal mediators for the more recent flocks of immigrants. Now it was the Irish who greeted the newly arrived at Ellis Island, stood up for immigrant worker's rights in unions, and became the role models for America's newest newcomers.

The United States is a land built in large part by immigrants. The Americans who harassed the Irish did not stop to think about the tremendous asset they were to the country. The Irish helped build the cities and bridges and canals and railroads and factories and schoolhouses. And immigrants from many countries provided America with the manpower it desperately needed to expand into one of the world's most powerful nations.

John F. Kennedy understood how vastly important immigration was to our country. In his book *A Nation of Immigrants*, Kennedy wrote:

The continuous immigration of the nineteenth and early twentieth centuries . . . gave every old American a standard by which to judge how far he had come and every new American a realization of how far he might go. It

Today, people of many nationalities help Irish Americans celebrate St. Patrick's Day

Library of Congress

reminded every American, old and new, that change is the essence of life, and that American society is a process, not a conclusion. . . . More than that, it infused the nation with a commitment to far horizons and new frontiers, and thereby kept the pioneer spirit of American life, the spirit of equality and of hope, always alive and strong.

Sadly, many ethnic groups still face discrimination in the United States. One would think, in "a nation of immigrants," that Americans would be especially sensitive to the problems and prejudices minorities encounter today. But many Americans have forgotten that diversity is what has been, and what will continue to be, our strength as a nation. By re-learning the history of our own ancestors, we can become more aware of the unfair prejudices that continue to plague our nation.

Today, more than 39 million Americans claim at least some Irish ancestry. For the most part (except for an occasional feisty, freckled redhead), Irish Americans are indistinguishable from the average American, and have overcome the prejudice they faced when they first arrived in America. Irish Americans are now represented in an endless variety of professions, be it as a publisher, priest, or president of the United States! Indeed, Orestes Brownson, a 19th-century writer who converted to Catholicism, was correct when he said of the Irish in 1854, "Out of these narrow lanes, blind courts, dirty streets, damp cellars, and suffocating garrets, will come forth some of the noblest sons of our country, whom she will delight to own and honor."

INDEX

Other books about Irish Americans:

Blumenthal, Shirley and Jerome S. Ozer. *Coming to America: Immigrants from the British Isles*. New York: Dell Publishing Co., Inc. 1980.

Cavan, Seamus. *Coming to America: The Irish-American Experience*. Brookfield, CT: The Millbrook Press, 1993.

Delaney, Mary Murray. *Of Irish Ways*. Minneapolis: Dillon Press, Inc., 1973.

Franck, Irene M. *The Irish-American Heritage*. New York: Facts on File, 1989.

Johnson, James E. *Irish in America*. New York: Lerner Publications Company, 1991.

Koustrup, Soren. *Ireland in Flight*. Mankato, MN: Creative Education, Inc., 1982.

Nardo, Don. *Irish Potato Famine*. San Diego: Lucent Books, 1990.

Wakin, Edward. *Enter the Irish-American*. New York: Thomas Y. Crowell Company, 1976.

JMP IS PROUD TO ANNOUNCE 4 NEW SERIES FOR YOUNG READERS AGES 8 AND UP

Watch for the arrival of these new series at your local bookstore. Or order direct by calling **1-800-888-7504** and receive our **free** young readers catalog.

BIZARRE & BEAUTIFUL SERIES

A spirited and fun investigation of the mysteries of the five senses in the animal kingdom.

Each title is 8¹/₂″ x 11″, 48 pages, $14.95 hardcover, with color photographs and illustrations throughout.

Bizarre & Beautiful Ears
Bizarre & Beautiful Eyes
Bizarre & Beautiful Feelers
Bizarre & Beautiful Noses
Bizarre & Beautiful Tongues

RAINBOW WARRIOR ARTISTS SERIES

W hat is a Rainbow Warrior Artist? It is a person who strives to live in harmony with the Earth and all living creatures, and who tries to better the world while living his or her life in a creative way.

Each title is written by Reavis Moore with a foreword by LeVar Burton, and is 8¹/₂″ x 11″, 48 pages, $14.95 hardcover, with color photographs and illustrations.

Native Artists of Africa (available 1/94)
Native Artists of North America

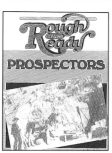
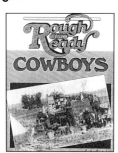

ROUGH AND READY SERIES

L earn about the men and women who settled the American frontier. Explore the myths and legends about these courageous individuals and learn about the environmental, cultural, and economic legacies they left to us.

Each title is written by A. S. Gintzler and is 48 pages, 8¹/₂″ x 11″, $12.95 hardcover, with two-color illustrations and duotone archival photographs.

Rough and Ready Cowboys (available 4/94)
Rough and Ready Homesteaders (available 4/94)
Rough and Ready Prospectors (available 4/94)

AMERICAN ORIGINS SERIES

M any of us are the third and fourth generation of our families to live in America. Learn what our great-great grandparents experienced when they arrived here and how much of our lives are still intertwined with theirs.

Each title is 48 pages, 8¹/₂″ x 11″, $12.95 hardcover, with two-color illustrations and duotone archival photographs.

Tracing Our German Roots, Leda Silver
Tracing Our Irish Roots, Sharon Moscinski
Tracing Our Italian Roots, Kathleen Lee
Tracing Our Jewish Roots, Miriam Sagan

ORDERING INFORMATION
Please check your local bookstore for our books, or call 1-800-888-7504 to order direct from us. All orders are shipped via UPS; see chart to calculate your shipping charge for U.S. destinations. **No P.O. Boxes please; we must have a street address to ensure delivery.** If the book you request is not available, we will hold your check until we can ship it. Foreign orders will be shipped surface rate unless otherwise requested; please enclose $3.00 for the first item and $1.00 for each additional item.

METHODS OF PAYMENT
Check, money order, American Express, MasterCard, or Visa. We cannot be responsible for cash sent through the mail. For credit card orders, include your card number, expiration date, and your signature, or call (800) 888-7504. American Express card orders can be shipped only to billing address of cardholder. Sorry, no C.O.D.'s. Residents of sunny New Mexico, add 6.125% tax to total.

Address all orders and inquiries to:
John Muir Publications
P.O. Box 613
Santa Fe, NM 87504
(505) 982-4078
(800) 888-7504

For U.S. Orders Totaling	Add
Up to $15.00	$4.25
$15.01 to $45.00	$5.25
$45.01 to $75.00	$6.25
$75.01 or more	$7.25

MORE OF YOUR FAVORITE JOHN MUIR PUBLICATIONS BOOKS
FOR A FREE CATALOG CALL 1-800-888-7504

EXTREMELY WEIRD SERIES

*A*ll of the titles are written by Sarah Lovett, 8½" x 11", 48 pages, $9.95 paperbacks, with color photographs and illustrations.

Extremely Weird Bats
Extremely Weird Birds
Extremely Weird Endangered Species
Extremely Weird Fishes
Extremely Weird Frogs
Extremely Weird Insects
Extremely Weird Mammals
Extremely Weird Micro Monsters
Extremely Weird Primates
Extremely Weird Reptiles
Extremely Weird Sea Creatures
Extremely Weird Snakes
Extremely Weird Spiders

X-RAY VISION SERIES

*E*ach title in the series is 8½" x 11", 48 pages, $9.95 paperback, with color photographs and illustrations and written by Ron Schultz.

Looking Inside the Brain
Looking Inside Cartoon Animation
Looking Inside Caves and Caverns
Looking Inside Sports Aerodynamics
Looking Inside Sunken Treasure
Looking Inside Telescopes and the Night Sky

THE KIDDING AROUND TRAVEL GUIDES

*A*ll of the titles listed below are 64 pages and $9.95 paperbacks, except for *Kidding Around the National Parks* and *Kidding Around Spain*, which are 108 pages and $12.95 paperbacks.

Kidding Around Atlanta
Kidding Around Boston, 2nd ed.
Kidding Around Chicago, 2nd ed.
Kidding Around the Hawaiian Islands
Kidding Around London
Kidding Around Los Angeles
Kidding Around the National Parks
  of the Southwest
Kidding Around New York City, 2nd ed.
Kidding Around Paris
Kidding Around Philadelphia
Kidding Around San Diego
Kidding Around San Francisco
Kidding Around Santa Fe
Kidding Around Seattle
Kidding Around Spain
Kidding Around Washington, D.C., 2nd ed.

MASTERS OF MOTION SERIES

*E*ach title in the series is 10¼" x 9", 48 pages, $9.95 paperback, with color photographs and illustrations.

How to Drive an Indy Race Car
  David Rubel
How to Fly a 747
  Tim Paulson
How to Fly the Space Shuttle
  Russell Shorto

THE KIDS EXPLORE SERIES

*E*ach title is written by kids for kids by the Westridge Young Writers Workshop, 7" x 9", with photographs and illustrations by the kids.

Kids Explore America's Hispanic Heritage
112 pages, $7.95 paper
Kids Explore America's African-American Heritage
128 pages, $8.95 paper
Kids Explore the Gifts of Children with Special Needs
112 pages, $8.95 paper (available 2/94)
Kids Explore America's Japanese Heritage
112 pages, $8.95 paper (available 4/94)

ENVIRONMENTAL TITLES

Habitats: Where the Wild Things Live
Randi Hacker and Jackie Kaufman
8½" x 11", 48 pages, color illustrations, $9.95 paper

The Indian Way: Learning to Communicate with Mother Earth
Gary McLain
7" x 9", 114 pages, illustrations, $9.95 paper

Rads, Ergs, and Cheeseburgers: The Kids' Guide to Energy and the Environment
Bill Yanda
7" x 9", 108 pages, two-color illustrations, $13.95 paper

The Kids' Environment Book: What's Awry and Why
Anne Pedersen
7" x 9", 192 pages, two-color illustrations, $13.95 paper